NATIONAL GEOGRAPHIC

Ladders

WELCOME TO BRAZIL
AROUND THE WORLD

Into the Rain Forest

by David Holford

Brazil is the largest country in South America. About half of Brazil is covered by the largest **rain forest** on Earth, the Amazon rain forest. Rain forests are warm and wet. They have many kinds of animals and plants. If you lived in a rain forest, you would always need to carry an umbrella. It rains almost every day.

Brazil's rain forest gets its name from the Amazon River. This river winds between the trees of the forest for many miles.

The Amazon rain forest is home to strange fish. The electric eel is a fish that looks like a snake. Its body stores up electric shocks. It zaps its enemies with these shocks!

More types of plants and animals live in the Amazon rain forest than any other place in the world. Most of the animals live in the **canopy**. The canopy is the layer of branches and leaves at the top of the forest. Chattering monkeys, colorful parrots, and lots of other animals live in the canopy. Many of them never even touch the forest floor.

A Home in the Forest

Many **tribes** live in the Amazon rain forest. A tribe is a group of people that shares the same language and beliefs. People from some tribes climb the trees and hunt the animals of the forest. One of these tribes is the Yanomami (yah-noh-MAH-mee).

The Yanomami live in villages throughout the forest. Several families live together. They share large, round houses built with vines and leaves. The men and older boys hunt monkeys, birds, and other animals for food. They hunt with bows and poison arrows.

Yanomami men and women plant gardens for food. The men chop down trees and other plants in small areas. Then they set the cuttings on fire. The burning clears the land to make room for gardens.

Once the clearing and burning is done, the women plant and tend the crops. The women's work is hard but important. Much of the tribe's food comes from gardens.

˅ This Yanomami girl wears flowers and paints her face for a celebration.

˅ Instead of a cat or a dog, this young Yanomami man keeps two parrots as pets.

This boy picked these bananas from a tree. The feathers on his head are from a parrot. The Yanomami get everything they need to live from the rain forest.

∧ Squirrel Monkey

∧ Red-and-Green Macaw

∧ Green Anaconda Snake

∧ Three-Toed Sloth

∨ Giant Anteater

∨ Pink River Dolphin

Respect the Rain Forest

The Yanomami treat the Amazon rain forest well. The forest gives them the things they need to live. They use plants and animals for food, clothing, and building homes. But the Yanomami take only what their families need to stay alive. They know that taking more than they need would hurt the rain forest.

Many Brazilians who live outside the rain forest feel the same as the Yanomami. They work hard to protect the rain forest from people who cut it down. Cutting down the rain forest destroys the homes of animals. It also wastes many useful plants that grow there. Some of these plants are used to make medicines that save lives.

People on vacation visit the Amazon rain forest to see the tall trees and colorful animals. These people can help protect the rain forest, too. They can be careful to leave no trace of their trip in the forest, just like the Yanomami.

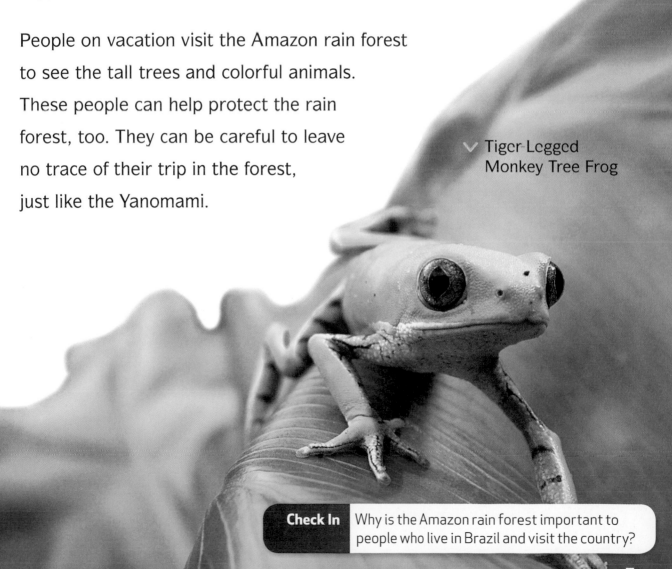

ˇ Tiger-Legged Monkey Tree Frog

Check In Why is the Amazon rain forest important to people who live in Brazil and visit the country?

Let's Go to Carnival!

by Hugh Westrup

> During each day of Carnival, more than 2 million people gather in the streets to celebrate. That's one big party!

It's Celebration Time

Imagine the Fourth of July, the Super Bowl, and Halloween all wrapped into one. In Brazil, people celebrate something like this each year during **Carnival** (kar-nuh-VAHL). They call Carnival "the biggest party on the planet."

Carnival is full of amazing sights. It's also full of toe-tapping music. For four days, people forget about work and school. They eat their favorite foods and dress in colorful costumes. They dance to the music of outdoor bands.

In the city of Rio de Janeiro (REE-oh day zhuh-NAIR-roh), the highlight of Carnival is a parade of floats. A float is a decorated platform on wheels that is pulled by a car. Each float is built by one of the city's **Samba** schools. Samba is a style of dance and a type of music. But a Samba school is not a place people go to learn. It's a club made up of neighbors. Each Samba school makes a fun, colorful float for Carnival.

> People spend thousands of hours painting a float. They use just as many gallons of paint.

⌃ A man makes a big flower for a float. This flower makes up one small part of a huge float.

It's a good thing grasshoppers aren't this big in real life!

Top-Secret Floats

Samba schools work all year to get ready for Carnival. Once Carnival ends, planning for the next year begins. Each Samba school has a **theme**, or big idea, for its float. Everything on the float relates to that theme. One theme might be about a special place in Brazil, such as the Amazon rain forest.

Floats are very big. They are put together inside huge buildings. Many people work together to build one float. For a float that shows the Amazon rain forest, carpenters might build a very large riverboat. Artists might make rain forest animals out of cloth and wire. They might make flowers out of paper and glue. Everything about the float is kept secret until Carnival. Each Samba school wants its float to be a surprise!

Get Up and Dance!

Samba music has quick drumbeats and lively horns. When you hear this music, it's impossible not to dance! Each Samba school chooses a new Samba song every year for Carnival. The dancers dance to this song during the parades. Before Carnival, the dancers practice their moves until they are ready to show off to the crowd.

Many people are needed to make the costumes for Carnival dancers and musicians. Every outfit is made by hand. For many months, sewing machines hum inside homes. Six miles of cloth, thousands of feathers, and millions of sparkling decorations called sequins make up the costumes for Carnival.

The colors of the costumes are bright. They might be flaming red, canary yellow, shocking pink, or peacock blue. But the costumes must be cool and comfortable to wear. Carnival is held in late February or early March, the warmest time of the year in Brazil.

> These dancers are wearing butterfly costumes. Because they are raised above the other performers, it looks like they are flying.

This woman is called the "Queen of Drums." She leads the drummers in the parade.

Dancers perform in groups called *wings*. Each wing has as many as 100 dancers. Everyone in the wing wears the same costume.

13

A float makes its way through a cheering crowd in the Sambadrome. Forty judges decide which float is the best.

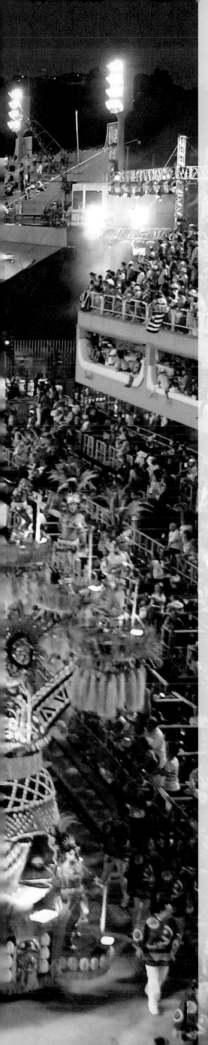

Parade Time

During Carnival, Samba schools show off their hard work in a place called the **Sambadrome**. This huge building has no roof. It's like an outdoor stage. A long road stretches down the middle of the building. The judges and crowds sit in bleachers on both sides of the road. As each Samba school enters the Sambadrome, the crowd claps their hands and cheers.

On the last two nights of Carnival, the 12 best Samba schools perform. Each school has 80 minutes to perform for the judges and crowd. First, the school's flag is carried into the Sambadrome. The drummers enter with a loud wave of sound from their instruments. Then the dancers shake and twirl to the band's music. They look like colorful birds.

Finally, the floats enter the Sambadrome. The crowd goes wild. This is what they have been waiting for. Only one Samba school can win the float contest. But no matter which school wins, the people of Rio de Janeiro have shown off their talents and imagination. They have put on one of the greatest shows on Earth!

Check In How does a community work together during Carnival?

GENRE Folk Tale

Read to find out about the Brazilian beetle.

How Beetle Got Her Coat

retold by Jenny Loomis

illustrated by Cecilia Rébora

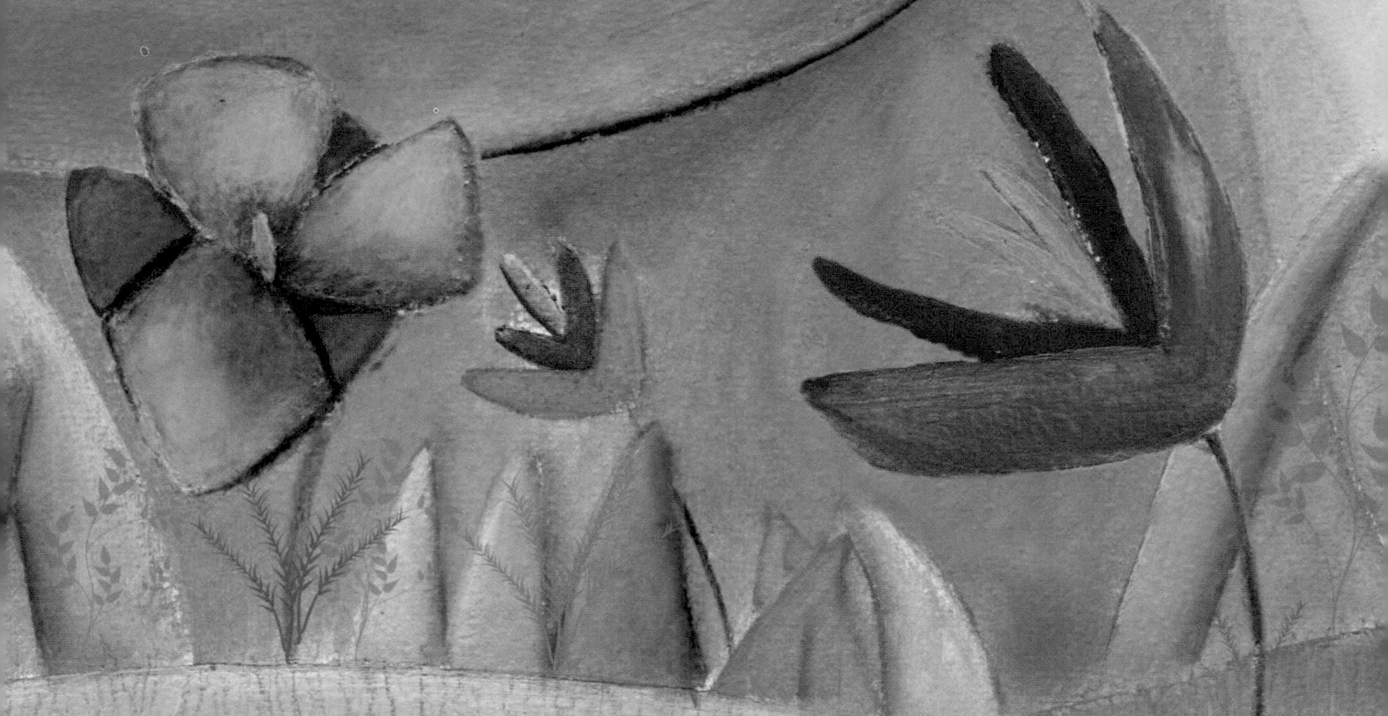

Long ago, different cultures made up stories to explain things they saw in nature. Why does an elephant have a long trunk? Why does a mosquito buzz? Why is the sky blue? These stories often used talking animals to teach lessons about how to behave. In this folk tale from Brazil, we find out how the Brazilian beetle got its colorful coat.

One hot afternoon, Beetle took a stroll through the rain forest. She loved to look at the orchids (AWR-kihdz) after the morning rains stopped. As she walked slowly along a dirt path, she smiled at the bright colors of the beautiful flowers. Their soft petals came in every shade of the rainbow. She especially liked the shiny blues and deep lime greens. Beetle looked at her own dull brown coat. She sighed, "If only my coat was as colorful as the orchids."

Suddenly, Beetle heard splashing coming from the river. She turned to see Rat swimming in her direction. He jumped out of the water and said, "Poor Beetle! How slowly you walk! It must take you forever to get anything done. Too bad you aren't more like me. I move so fast I'll make your head spin. Watch!"

Beetle rolled her eyes and kept walking. She found it best to ignore Rat when he started bragging.

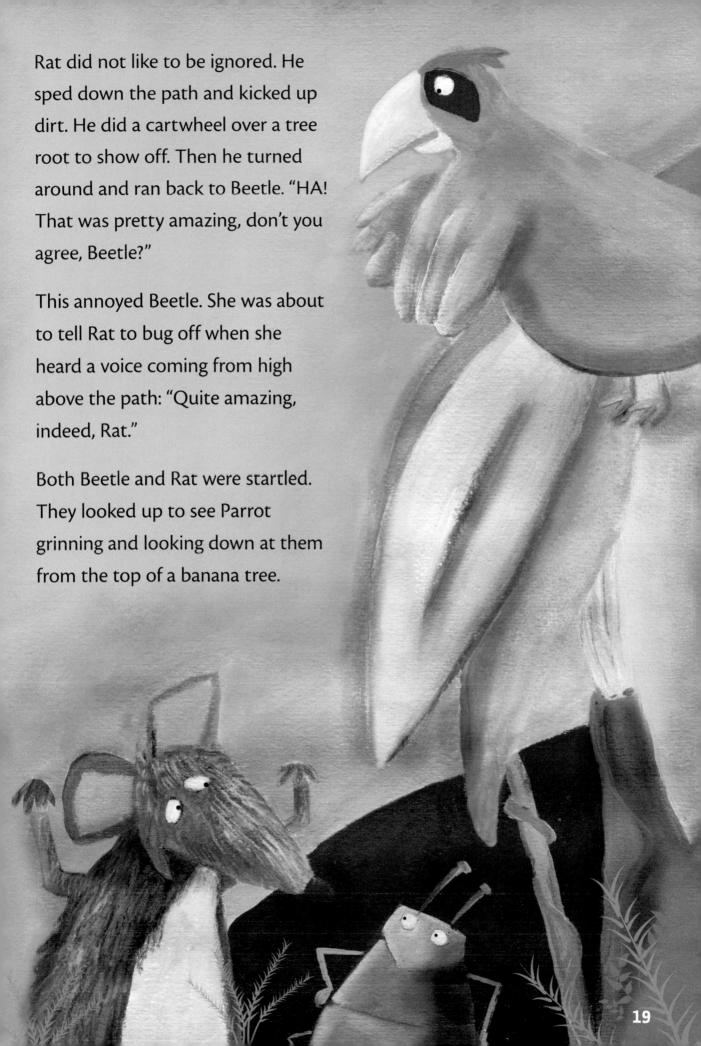

Rat did not like to be ignored. He sped down the path and kicked up dirt. He did a cartwheel over a tree root to show off. Then he turned around and ran back to Beetle. "HA! That was pretty amazing, don't you agree, Beetle?"

This annoyed Beetle. She was about to tell Rat to bug off when she heard a voice coming from high above the path: "Quite amazing, indeed, Rat."

Both Beetle and Rat were startled. They looked up to see Parrot grinning and looking down at them from the top of a banana tree.

"Your speed gives me an idea for a race. The prize will be a beautiful coat in any color the winner likes. Interested?" asked Parrot.

Rat jumped with excitement. "Oh, this is great! I'm finally going to have a shiny black coat like Panther! No one notices how fast I am because my brown and white coat is so boring. Once I get a black coat, the other animals will give me the attention I deserve. Let's start this race," squeaked Rat.

The thought of a new colorful coat made Beetle happy, too. She also agreed to the race.

"Terrific! The first animal to reach that large nut tree is the winner. Ready? GO!" yelled Parrot.

Rat ran as fast as he could without looking behind him. He kept thinking about how handsome he would look in his new black coat. He did a joyful dance when he got to the tree. Looking around for Parrot, Rat announced, "I won, Parrot! I want my shiny black coat now!"

Rat looked up at the nut tree, and couldn't believe what he saw. Sitting next to Parrot was Beetle wearing a sparkling blue and green coat.

"How did you get here so fast, Beetle? I didn't see you pass me," asked Rat angrily.

"I flew up here," replied Beetle.

"Flew? I didn't know you could fly!" yelled Rat.

"Rat, you don't know anything about me. The only time you talk to me is when you're making fun of me," explained Beetle. "You thought I looked slow and helpless. But you were wrong."

Rat angrily kicked the nut tree, shaking a Brazil nut loose. It fell on his head.

From that day on, Beetle proudly wore her fancy blue and green coat in the rain forest. She was as colorful as the orchids she loved so much.

Rat had his same old coat, but he changed in other ways. Rat stopped judging the other animals by how they looked—especially the ones he thought he might have to race one day!

Check In Why did Rat think that Beetle could not win the race?

Discuss

1. What connections can you make among the three selections that you read in this book?

2. In what ways do the Yanomami people depend on the Amazon rain forest? What could happen to their way of life if the rain forest is not protected?

3. Tell about the tradition of Carnival in Brazil. Describe how a tradition in your country is similar to Carnival.

4. Folk tales often use animals to teach lessons about how to behave. What lessons did you learn by reading this folk tale?

5. What do you still wonder about life in Brazil?